The Great Aussie Tradie Nickname Compendium

by
Bobbie Butler

Copyright © 2023 Bobbie Butler
All rights reserved.
ISBN: 978-0-9925034-9-9

CONTENTS

Contents	i
Introduction	1
Nicknames for the Workmates Who Are Just Lazy	3
Nicknames for the Workmates Who Are Just Hopeless	9
Nicknames for the Workmates Because of a Condition or Habit They Have	14
Nicknames for the Workmates Who Hardly Show Up	18
Nicknames for the Workmates Who Are Rubbish at Their Job	22
Nicknames for the Workmates Who No-one Really Likes	25
Acknowledgements	28

Welcome to "The Great Aussie Tradie Nickname Compendium," your trusty guide through the colourful world of Australian job site nicknames. We've scoured the internet for as many names as we could find.

This book isn't just a list; it's an exploration into the camaraderie and humour that make the Australian trades so unique.

From 'Chippie' to 'Sparkie,' the nicknames that are more than mere labels—they're badges of honour, jokes between mates, and sometimes, even terms of endearment.

So, step into the lively and spirited world of Australian tradies.

Nicknames for the Workmates Who Are Just Lazy

Wicket-keeper – puts on the gloves and stands back.

Sensor Light – only works if someone walks past.

Wheelbarrow – only works when pushed.

Cordless – charges all night but only works for 2 hours.

English Fog – someone who won't lift.

Muffler – someone who is always exhausted.

Cane Toad – every time he stops working he sits down.

Devondale – someone who always does the cream jobs.

Paper Straw – someone who works but not for long.

The Ornament – all he does is stand around doing nothing.

Blister – appears after all the hard work is done.

Brake Pad – gets worn out easily then starts to squeal.

Bollard – just stands around all day.

Morphine – slow-moving dope.

2-Stroke – hard to start and always smoking.

Pothole – always in the road.

Harvey Norman – it's been 3 years with no interest.

Mastercard – always takes credit for someone else's work.

Noodles – thinks all jobs take 2 minutes.

Hostage – someone who is always tied up with something.

Grenade – always waiting for him to pull the pin.

Egon – where has he gone again?

Trapdoor – comes out and grabs anyone who walks past his way for a gossip.

10mm Socket – can never be found when you need him.

Justin – does 'just en'ough not to get fired.

Scaff – always hanging around the job not really doing any work.

Bushranger – always holding everyone up.

Broken Arrow – doesn't work and can't be fired.

Sandbag – he just leans on the barriers all day.

Roomba – moves around a lot but barely picks up anything.

Mushroom – a 'fun-gi' but hangs around doing nothing.

Computer – goes to sleep if left unattended for 15 minutes.

KitKat - always taking a break.

Nicknames for the Workmates Who Are Just Hopeless

Seaweed – just floats around all day and stinks.

.... ⛑ ....

Show Bag – full of shit.

.... ⛑ ....

Deck Chair – always folds under pressure.

.... ⛑ ....

Perth – he's always 3 hours behind everyone else.

.... ⛑ ....

Kinder Surprise – melts in the heat.

.... ⛑ ....

Glow Stick – he needs shaking for the lights to come on.

.... ⛑ ....

Fire Drill – causes a lot of movement for no real reason.

.... ⛑ ....

Skittles – because he's not a bloody smarty.

.... ⛑ ....

Cold Sore – no matter how much crap you put on them, they keep coming back.

.... ⛑ ....

Pluto – far out and not very bright.

Bottle – empty from the neck up.

Lantern – not very bright, and always has to be carried.

Butterknife – not the sharpest tool in the box.

Drill bit – he's a small boring tool.

Rainforest – just thick and dense.

Thomas the Tank Engine – he goes hard but runs out of steam.

Chainsaw – hard to start and stops for no reason

Cyclone – a slow moving depression.

Tail Light – not bright enough to be up the front.

· ⛑ ·

Bungalow – nothing upstairs.

· ⛑ ·

Exorcist – every time he leaves your house all the spirits are gone.

· ⛑ ·

Sundial – only works when the sun is out.

· ⛑ ·

Sandpaper – always abrasive and difficult to work with.

· ⛑ ·

1 Grit – as rough as they come.

· ⛑ ·

Wi-Fi – full bars but no connection.

· ⛑ ·

Nicknames for the Workmates Because of a Condition or Habit They Have

Winchester – thinks he's an absolute gun at everything.

Glass Eye – looks effective but doesn't do much.

Mirrors – he 's always 'looking into it'.

Damplamps – he's got runny eye's.

Limo – carries 8 other people.

Turbo – always works at high speed.

2pac – smokes 40 cigarettes a day.

Rust – gets in everyone's car.

Bluey - he's got red hair.

Sauce - he's got red hair.

Mortgage Eyes – because one is fixed and one is variable.

TikTok – one arm shorter than the other.

The Dunker – coz he's got gingernuts.

Keth – his name is Keith and he is missing an eye.

Uzi – he has a wonky eye, 'uzi looking at?'

Ten to Two – his feet point outwards.

Kellogs – he looks like a cereal killer.

Dulux – he always wears two coats.

Summer Teeth – summer green, summer brown, summer missing

Jurassic Spark – he's the oldest electrician on site

Nicknames for the Workmates Who Hardly Show Up

G-Spot – you can never find him.

Golf Ball – he's also hard to find.

Halftime – only there half the time.

Easter Bunny – four day long weekend, every weekend.

Dodo – day on day off.

Mirage – you only see him in the right conditions.

The Hurricane – blows hard for a while then disappears.

ET – just wants to go home.

Cinderella – he's always gone by 12.

Garbo – only shows up once a week.

Daisies – some days he's there, some days he's not.

Fuxy – "Where the fuxy gone now?"

Ghost – never know when he is going to show up and always shocked when he does.

China – he only comes out on special occasions.

Eclipse – only shows rarely, and everyone stops to look.

Nicknames for the Workmates Who Are Rubbish at Their Job

The Moth – Crane driver on oil rig kept hitting the lights.

The Reverend – excavator driver who never missed an underground utility service.

Audi – chippie puts 4 circles around every nail.

Depth Charge – always asking for a sub.

Duct Tape – always patching up his mistakes.

Apple Maps – always steers you in the wrong direction.

Bandaid – he's always covering up mistakes.

Lightning – someone who can never hit the same spot twice.

Nicknames for the Workmates Who No-one Really Likes

Toes – so far up the boss's arse, all you can see are his toes.

- - -

Stingray – stands around with hands on hips (aka safety officers).

- - -

Dogshit – because no one likes picking him up.

- - -

Shania – he don't impress you much.

- - -

Feta – he always crumbles under pressure.

- - -

Platypus – boss's son. Protected species.

- - -

Slinky – good for nothing but fun to push down the stairs.

- - -

Splinter – annoying little prick that gets under your skin.

- - -

Bomb-scare – nothing empties a room faster than him showing up.

Rucksack – for the manager, he's always on your back.

Pothole – everyone tries to avoid him.

8 Gauge – he's thick and difficult to work with.

The Pandemic – he just won't fuck off.

Acknowledgements

These nicknames have been collected from various pages, podcasts, videos and comments from various platforms that had also collated these from individual contributers. No one source was the main source of this collection and many of these nicknames are repeated in numerous variations across the internet.

We know that many of you tradies out there are women, but for sake of brevity we've just used 'he', so soz Tradie Ladies.

We have used ai for the illustrations in this book because Bobbie Butler is a one year old Moodle who works for Butler Diaries Pty Ltd and cannot draw. This is her first foray in to publishing - we think she has done quite well.

www.ingramcontent.com/pod-product-compliance
Lightning Source LLC
Chambersburg PA
CBHW070443010526
44118CB00014B/2170